Who Was
Queen Elizabeth?

By June Eding

Illustrated by Nancy Harrison

Grosset & Dunlap

For two other very regal redheads, Phoebe and Leah—J.E.
To women who persevere—N.H.

GROSSET & DUNLAP
Published by the Penguin Group
Penguin Group (USA) Inc., 375 Hudson Street, New York, New York 10014, USA
Penguin Group (Canada), 90 Eglinton Avenue East, Suite 700, Toronto,
Ontario M4P 2Y3, Canada (a division of Pearson Penguin Canada Inc.)
Penguin Books Ltd., 80 Strand, London WC2R 0RL, England
Penguin Group Ireland, 25 St. Stephen's Green, Dublin 2, Ireland
(a division of Penguin Books Ltd.)
Penguin Group (Australia), 250 Camberwell Road, Camberwell, Victoria 3124, Australia
(a division of Pearson Australia Group Pty. Ltd.)
Penguin Books India Pvt. Ltd., 11 Community Centre, Panchsheel Park,
New Delhi—110 017, India
Penguin Group (NZ), 67 Apollo Drive, Rosedale, North Shore 0632, New Zealand
(a division of Pearson New Zealand Ltd.)
Penguin Books (South Africa) (Pty.) Ltd., 24 Sturdee Avenue,
Rosebank, Johannesburg 2196, South Africa

Penguin Books Ltd., Registered Offices: 80 Strand, London WC2R 0RL, England

Library of Congress Control Number: 2007045387

ISBN 978-0-448-44839-8   30 29 28 27 26 25 24 23 22 21

Who Was
Queen Elizabeth?

Contents

Who Was
Queen Elizabeth?

England, August 1588. A fleet of powerful Spanish warships is sailing toward England. The Spanish fleet, called the Armada, has 130 mighty ships. Each is heavily armed. Their goal is to invade

the island-nation. King Philip of Spain wants to be king of England as well.

But England's ruler is brave and fearless. She is Queen Elizabeth. She does not intend to let the Spanish king take her throne.

Her soldiers are waiting on the coast of England. They are ready to defend their country. The queen's advisers do not want her anywhere near a

battle. They worry about her safety.

But Elizabeth does not listen.

The queen sets off on horseback from London to where the soldiers have set up camp. Elizabeth wants to be with her men. If there is a battle, words from the queen herself will help lead her men to victory.

The queen rides up on a great horse. She passes among the crowd of soldiers. She wants everyone to hear words spoken from her heart.

The queen says she is there "to live or die amongst you." Elizabeth is telling her soldiers that, even though she is queen, she is willing to die with them. She ends by saying, "I know I have the body of but a weak and feeble woman, but I have the heart and stomach of a king, and of a king of England, too."

With tears in her eyes, the queen promises, "We shall shortly have a famous victory" over our enemies.

And she is right. The English ships are smaller than the Spanish ships. But they set many Spanish ships on fire and break up the enemy fleet. And the English also get lucky—there is very bad weather. Spanish ships try to flee and instead crash against England's rocky shore. They are destroyed.

England is saved. People throughout the country rejoice. They call their brave Elizabeth "Good Queen Bess."

For the rest of her life and long after her death, Elizabeth's faithful and loving people would rejoice that she was their queen.

Chapter 1
Young Elizabeth

On September 7, 1533, a baby girl was born in a palace in Greenwich, England. Her father was King Henry the Eighth, a handsome man who loved to hunt, to eat and drink, and to be in the company of beautiful women. Her mother, Queen Anne, was young and very beautiful indeed. The baby had her father's bright red hair and pale skin.

ANNE BOLEYN

When she was only three days old, the little princess was brought to church. She wore a long dress of silk and lace. Over it, a tiny robe trimmed in fur kept her warm. One of the king's officers announced her arrival—"the high and mighty" Princess Elizabeth. It was a very grand occasion.

The truth, however, was that Elizabeth's father was not at all happy over her birth. King Henry wanted a child of his to rule after him. But he did not want Elizabeth to be queen. Certainly a woman could not rule a country all by herself! Besides, Henry already had one daughter from his first marriage. Princess Mary was now seventeen years old.

MARY TUDOR

Queen Anne had promised Henry a boy. That's what Henry wanted. And Henry was a man who expected to get what he wanted. If he didn't, there could be big trouble.

And soon there was. After the little princess was born, Henry was convinced that Queen Anne would never bear a son. So he accused her of a crime she did not commit. Anne was put on trial and sentenced to death. Elizabeth was not even three years old when her mother was beheaded. Now King Henry was free to marry again. And within two weeks of Anne's death, he did. Luckily for the new queen, she gave birth to a baby boy. His name was Edward.

KING HENRY THE EIGHTH

What did this mean for little Elizabeth? It meant she was no longer important. In her father's eyes, she was no longer even a princess. She was sent away to a palace far from London. She hardly ever saw her father.

Fortunately, Elizabeth had many loving people to look after her. There was her governess Catherine, called "Cat." Elizabeth and Cat stayed friends long after Elizabeth grew up. Cat made sure that Elizabeth was happy and healthy. She also made sure that the king sent enough money for Elizabeth's needs—food and clothes and books.

Another important person in Elizabeth's life was Roger Ascham. He was Elizabeth's private teacher. Although most girls in the 1500s had no schooling, Elizabeth was the daughter of a king. She was expected

to read and write.

Young Elizabeth was a quick learner. Ascham called her "the brightest star" of all the girls he taught. Elizabeth studied math, history, literature, astronomy, and geography. She especially loved to read and would spend hours with books in Greek and Latin. By the time she was a teenager, Elizabeth knew five languages besides English: French, Italian, Spanish, Greek, and Latin. Sometimes she and Ascham would speak to each other in Greek or Latin.

Elizabeth learned to play an instrument called the virginal. It was like a piano. She started sewing when she was six and  became very good at needlework. Other tutors instructed Elizabeth in horseback riding and

AN EMBROIDERED BAG

dancing. There wasn't much time for play. And, like all children of that time, Elizabeth was expected to act like a tiny adult.

Every once in a while, young Elizabeth would overhear gossip. Henry's third wife had died. Then he divorced his next wife and beheaded the one after that. It was very risky for a woman to be married to King Henry!

As the years went by, Elizabeth grew into a serious, intelligent teenager. In a portrait of Elizabeth at the age of thirteen, she wears a simple yet beautiful red dress. It is one of the only portraits of young Elizabeth. A book lies open on a stand behind her. She is holding another book. Her finger marks the page. It seems as if she plans to start reading again as soon as the artist is finished painting! Despite growing up with no mother or

father, Elizabeth was becoming an elegant and talented young woman.

What Elizabeth did not know was that she would become the most important person in England. And it wouldn't be long before people—powerful people—would want her dead.

Chapter 2
The Princess Is a Prisoner

When Elizabeth was thirteen, her father died. Prince Edward was only nine. Still, he became king. Sadly, Edward was often sick, and died at the age of fifteen. Princess Mary, the oldest of Henry's three children, now became queen.

Mary was already thirty-seven years old. Within a year, the new queen married Prince Philip of Spain. Like Mary, Philip was Catholic. The Catholic religion was very important to Mary. And she insisted that everyone else in England

KING EDWARD

be Catholic as well. Those who didn't obey could be put to death. During her rule, more than 250 people were burned at the stake.

The English people hated Mary. They called her "Bloody Mary." Also, they resented that Mary had married Philip. They did not want a Spanish prince to have so much power over their country.

As for Queen Mary, she resented her half sister Elizabeth. She always had. After all, King Henry had divorced Mary's mother to marry Elizabeth's mother.

Mary also did not trust Elizabeth. She thought Elizabeth was plotting to be queen. So she had Elizabeth thrown in jail.

On a cold and rainy night, Elizabeth was sent by boat to the Tower of London. She was only nineteen years old. The boat passed under London Bridge. Above her, the heads of traitors were displayed on poles. Did the same fate await Elizabeth?

The boat arrived at the steps that led up to her prison cell. At first, Elizabeth would not go. She knew there was no escape. But she wanted to make it clear to everyone that her punishment was not fair. She was innocent. So she sat down on the cold, wet stone steps. When she felt she had made her point, she rose and climbed to her cell.

Elizabeth remained there for two months,

never knowing from one day to the next if Mary
planned to kill her. Elizabeth wrote to her sister
Mary, declaring her innocence. But her letters
were ignored.

Finally Queen Mary released Elizabeth. Still,
she had to live under house arrest for a year at a
nearby palace. Elizabeth was watched closely. She
learned to keep her thoughts to herself.

As for Queen Mary, she was desperately trying
to have a baby. She wanted to raise a Catholic
child, one who would rule after her and make
sure England stayed Catholic. But she remained
childless. Then, her health started to fail.

THE TOWER OF LONDON

ALMOST A THOUSAND YEARS OLD AND ONCE SURROUNDED BY A MOAT, THE TOWER WAS ORIGINALLY BUILT TO PROTECT THE CITY FROM INVADERS. OVER THE YEARS, THE TOWER OF LONDON GREW TO INCLUDE MANY BUILDINGS. AT ONE POINT THERE WAS EVEN A ZOO WITHIN THE TOWER YARD! BUT THE TOWER IS MOST FAMOUS FOR BEING A PRISON.

MANY PRISONERS ARRIVED BY BOAT, PASSING THROUGH "TRAITORS' GATE." MANY FAMOUS NAMES IN ENGLISH HISTORY SPENT THEIR LAST DAYS AT THE TOWER. ELIZABETH'S OWN MOTHER WAS SENT TO THE TOWER AND BEHEADED IN A PRIVATE COURTYARD.

TODAY, THE TOWER OF LONDON IS A POPULAR TOURIST ATTRACTION. THE CROWN JEWELS—NECKLACES, RINGS, CROWNS, AND TIARAS THAT BELONG TO BRITISH KINGS AND QUEENS—ARE KEPT THERE ON DISPLAY.

Queen Mary was forced to face the facts: Elizabeth would be queen after her. Still, Mary waited until she was on her deathbed to declare Elizabeth the new queen. It was November 17, 1558.

Elizabeth was reading under an oak tree when two officers of the court rode up to her. One of the men presented Elizabeth with the royal ring. It was the one that Mary had worn. Elizabeth said a prayer of gratitude in Latin. She had survived Mary's rule. Now she was queen. Elizabeth was only twenty-five years old.

From now on, she would answer to only one person: herself.

Elizabeth was crowned queen of England on January 15, 1559, in a famous London church called Westminster Abbey.

Elizabeth wore a beautiful golden gown and a matching robe trimmed in white fur. As she sat on her throne, parts of the Bible were read aloud. This was to show that Elizabeth was a queen in God's eyes, too. Her power could not be questioned.

In a portrait painted in honor of that day, Elizabeth has a scepter in her right hand. The scepter is a symbol of authority. In her left hand, she holds an orb. The way her hand grasps the orb is meant to show that her power reaches all over the world. In the painting, Elizabeth's long red hair is flowing. Her cheeks are slightly flushed. The new queen looks young and full of life.

Already Elizabeth had learned a great deal. She knew how people close to her could turn against her. She would have to be careful and smart if she was going to remain queen.

Chapter 3
The Young Queen

The English people loved Elizabeth. On her first day as queen, she was carried through the streets of London in a great parade. Despite the cold, everyone in the city gathered outside. People cheered. Church bells rang. Colorful flags and banners fluttered along her route. Music groups and troupes of actors performed on special stages as the queen passed by.

Elizabeth stopped again and again to greet people and thank them.

THE QUEEN'S PROGRESS

ELIZABETH
LIKED TO MEET
AND GREET
HER PEOPLE.
MOST PEOPLE
LIVED IN THE
COUNTRYSIDE.
SO EVERY
SUMMER, THE QUEEN

LEFT LONDON AND TOOK A LONG TRIP, VISITING
DIFFERENT TOWNS THROUGHOUT ENGLAND. SHE
MUST HAVE ENJOYED ESCAPING FROM LONDON,
WHICH WAS CROWDED, SMELLY, AND OFTEN
UNHEALTHY IN THE SUMMER.

THE QUEEN DID NOT PACK LIGHTLY. SHE
TRAVELED WITH MORE THAN 400 WAGONS AND
2,500 PACKHORSES!

ALONG HER ROUTE, THE QUEEN STOPPED TO
GREET HER PEOPLE. ELIZABETH ALWAYS FOUND
A WAY TO SHOW HER LOVE FOR THEM. ONCE,
SHE STOOD IN THE RAIN TO WATCH A LITTLE BOY
PERFORM FOR HER.

ELIZABETH STAYED AT THE HOMES OF THE
NOBILITY. EACH FAMILY TRIED ITS HARDEST TO

IMPRESS THE QUEEN. PLAYS, BANQUETS, AND
FIREWORKS WOULD GO ON FOR DAYS! THIS WAS
COSTLY FOR NOBLE FAMILIES BUT WORTH THE
HONOR OF PLAYING HOST TO THE QUEEN.

Later there was a great banquet at Whitehall Palace. All members of the court were invited— 800 guests attended! Dancing and feasting went on for hours. At one point a knight rode into the hall on his horse. To show his love for the queen, he threw down his glove. That act was a challenge. If any knight was disloyal to the queen, he had to fight the knight on horseback. No one wanted to fight, of course.

The next day, Elizabeth awoke in Whitehall Palace. It was just one of her new homes. She had many different palaces all over England. But most of her time was spent at Whitehall Palace. Whitehall was already hundreds of years old. But Elizabeth's father had made improvements, adding arenas for tournaments and cockfights as well as tennis courts.

Nevertheless the rough stone walls of the castle made the rooms cold and damp. The only warmth came from roaring fires in giant fireplaces (there was no electricity, running water, or modern heat systems back then). Even during the day, rooms were dark. There were no large windows, because they let in drafts. Also, glass was expensive. Hundreds of candles were needed to provide light during the day as well as at night.

Still, Elizabeth lived a life of luxury compared with that of her subjects. Most people worked on farms in the countryside and lived in two-room homes. Brick and stone were expensive, so the walls and roofs of the houses were strengthened with a mixture of clay and straw. Straw roofs kept houses warm, but they could catch fire easily. Rats

and other creatures often made their homes in the straw, too!

It was hard work just to survive. Because there was no electricity, people awoke with the sunrise and worked until nightfall. Anything that could not be grown or made by hand was bought at the weekly town market. Families—even young children—shared household chores.

The queen certainly did not have to do chores! She had servants. Lots of servants. It took many people to keep a castle running. Wood was brought in for the fires. Water was pumped from wells and carried inside. A team of cooks and kitchen workers prepared the royal meals.

The queen had servants to clean up after her. She had servants to make her bed, clean her room, and empty her chamber pot. (There was no plumbing for toilets.)

Practically wherever she went, Elizabeth was surrounded by her "ladies-in-waiting." These were young, unmarried women from noble families. It was their job to take care of all the queen's personal needs. They bathed and dressed her. They kept her company while she read or played music. It was a great honor to be a lady-in-waiting—no payment was given.

It might seem to the average person that the queen had an easy life. But Elizabeth said, to "wear a crown is more glorious to them that see it than it is a pleasure to them that bear it." What she meant was that being a ruler—the person who wore the crown—was difficult. She knew her citizens depended on her for their safety and well-being, to protect them from enemies.

As queen, Elizabeth had a great deal of power. The queen could make laws and declare wars. However, a lot of money was needed. Money came through taxes. To raise taxes, Elizabeth had to consult parliament. Parliament was made up of the House of Commons (members from the lower classes, or "common" people), and the House of Lords (made up of bishops and noblemen). Elizabeth decided when to meet with parliament and what would be discussed. In all the forty-four years she was queen, she called parliament into session only ten times. Instead she relied on a group of advisers. They made up the Privy Council.

THE PRIVY COUNCIL

ON IMPORTANT MATTERS, ELIZABETH TURNED TO A GROUP OF MEN KNOWN AS THE PRIVY COUNCIL. THEY GAVE THE KING OR QUEEN ADVICE ABOUT WAR, TAXES, AND NEWS OF OTHER COUNTRIES—WHICH RULERS WERE FRIENDLY TO ENGLAND AND WHICH WEREN'T.

THE SECRETARY OF STATE WAS THE MOST IMPORTANT PERSON ON THE PRIVY COUNCIL. ELIZABETH CHOSE WILLIAM CECIL FOR THE JOB. CECIL HAD BEEN ELIZABETH'S ACCOUNTANT, AND THE TWO WERE GREAT FRIENDS. TOGETHER, ELIZABETH AND CECIL BECAME A POWERFUL TEAM. HE WAS THIRTY-EIGHT YEARS OLD WHEN HE STARTED WORKING FOR THE QUEEN, AND HE REMAINED WITH HER FOR FORTY YEARS, UNTIL THE DAY HE

WILLIAM CECIL

DIED. ELIZABETH ALWAYS DEMANDED THE TRUTH FROM CECIL, EVEN IF IT WAS BAD NEWS.

BEING QUEEN PRESENTED DANGER. THERE HAD BEEN MANY PLOTS AGAINST QUEEN MARY. ALTHOUGH ELIZABETH WAS FAR MORE POPULAR

THAN MARY, SHE KNEW SHE HAD ENEMIES.

ONE MEMBER OF ELIZABETH'S PRIVY COUNCIL, SIR FRANCIS WALSINGHAM, SERVED AS HER "EYES AND EARS." ELIZABETH WANTED TO KNOW EVERYTHING, AND WALSINGHAM HAD SPIES ALL OVER EUROPE. HE PAID THEM FOR ANY NEWS OF PLOTS AGAINST THE QUEEN. ELIZABETH DID NOT REALLY LIKE WALSINGHAM, BUT WALSINGHAM WAS VERY LOYAL TO HER. HE EVEN SPENT HIS OWN MONEY TO PAY FOR THE SPIES.

SIR FRANCIS WALSINGHAM

Just as her father had, Elizabeth slept in a bedroom right next to the room where the Council met. Many times Elizabeth called the Council in the middle of the night. Her advisers had to be ready at any moment to serve their queen.

Chapter 4
Always the Same

What was the country that Elizabeth ruled like? England in the mid-1500s was weak and unstable. The treasury did not have much money. Powerful countries like Spain and France were a threat. Spain, especially, had rich colonies in the New World.

Also, since the time of Henry the Eighth, a great deal of blood had been shed over the question of religion.

As queen, Elizabeth decided how the English people should worship God. People had to worship in the same way the king or queen did—or there could be big trouble.

When Elizabeth's father, Henry, was born, the Catholic Church was thought to be the one true church in all of Europe. The pope, who headed the Catholic Church, was very powerful—more powerful than a king. However, in the 1500s, people started to break away from the Catholic Church. They formed new churches. In Germany, the Protestant movement took root.

In England, Henry the Eighth decided to break away from the Catholic Church. Why? Because he wanted a divorce. Henry desperately wanted to get rid of his first wife and remarry so he might have a son. But Catholics were not allowed to get a divorce—not even the king. Henry's solution was to start his own church: the Church of England. Who would be the head of the new church? Why, Henry himself! And his new church would allow divorces.

After Henry's daughter Mary became queen, she forced England to return to the Catholic Church. Many of those who refused were burned at the stake, often in front of crowds.

THE REFORMATION

MARTIN LUTHER

ON OCTOBER 31, 1517, A MONK NAMED MARTIN LUTHER NAILED A PIECE OF PAPER TO A CHURCH DOOR IN GERMANY FOR ALL TO SEE. LUTHER HAD WRITTEN DOWN A LIST OF COMPLAINTS AGAINST THE CATHOLIC CHURCH: THE POPE HAD TOO MUCH POWER; OFFICIALS TOOK MONEY FOR THE CHURCH FROM THE POOR AND SPENT IT ON THEMSELVES. LUTHER WANTED TO CHANGE THE WAY CATHOLIC CHURCHES IN EUROPE PRACTICED RELIGION. "REFORM" IS ANOTHER WORD FOR "CHANGE." THAT'S WHY THIS MOVEMENT IS CALLED THE REFORMATION.

Now that Elizabeth was queen, what would she do about religion in England?

She belonged to the Church of England. So within four months of being crowned, Elizabeth ordered that all English citizens be members of the Church of England. But, she said, she did not want to make "windows into men's souls." This meant she did not need to know exactly how everyone felt about God. As long as her people were loyal, the queen would not use violence to change their beliefs. The days of Bloody Mary were over for good.

Elizabeth had a hot temper. From her very first meetings with the Privy Council, it was clear that Elizabeth expected to get her way—always. During meetings, she would often pound her fist on the table. She shouted at advisers who disagreed with her. Elizabeth did not mind behaving "unwomanly." She swore more than many of her men. The rooms of Whitehall Castle

echoed with her commanding voice.

More importantly, Elizabeth was clever at making people do what she wanted them to do. She understood human nature. If a Council member was upset over something, she led him to believe another Council member was responsible for the problem, not the queen. She played her advisers against one another. Many became bitter rivals. Usually they were too busy arguing with one another to argue with the queen.

Elizabeth sometimes frustrated her advisers. If an enemy country were plotting against England, members of the Privy Council would want to act—fast—and send soldiers into battle. Elizabeth did not like to make sudden, big decisions. Her experiences had taught her that change was not always for the good. Her motto, in Latin, was *semper eadem*—"always the same."

Chapter 5
Marriage?

One question that Elizabeth avoided was marriage. Her Privy Council expected her to marry. Elizabeth wanted to remain single. She said, "It is monstrous that the feet should direct the head." By that she meant that the Privy Council, who was beneath her (the "feet"), could not tell her (the "head") what to do.

In 1559, King Philip of Spain asked to marry Elizabeth. He had married her sister Queen Mary in hopes of expanding his vast empire. Now Mary was dead. It was still in Spain's interest for Philip to marry England's new queen. Royalty did not marry for love. They married for power. If two people from two countries wed, their countries united. Philip expected to take control of England after

PHILIP OF SPAIN

his marriage to Elizabeth.

Elizabeth turned Philip down. She valued her independence. She saw many reasons not to marry him, or anyone else. From her father's marriages, she understood how quickly a king could make a queen a prisoner—or put her to death. If Elizabeth became pregnant, there was a great risk of her dying in childbirth. She told her advisers that even had she been born a poor milkmaid, she would rather stay single than marry a rich king.

Still, the proposals kept coming in. From the moment she was crowned, kings and royalty from all over Europe wanted a chance to woo the queen—and rule England.

Although she did not want any man making

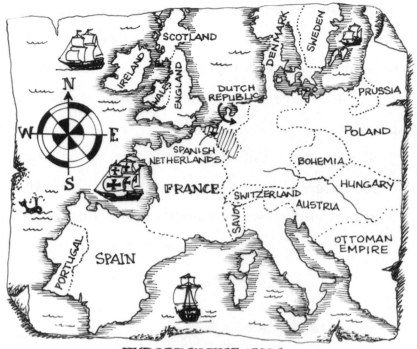

EUROPE IN THE 1500S

decisions for her, Elizabeth was smart enough to pretend to be interested in a husband.

In this way, she kept the Privy Council happy. It also kept rulers of other countries from waging war against England. No man was going to invade England if Elizabeth might say yes to his proposal.

So, did Elizabeth ever fall in love? To this day, no one knows for sure. If Elizabeth could have married for love, many historians believe she would have chosen Robert Dudley, Earl of Leicester.

Robert and Elizabeth had met when they were children. Like Elizabeth, Robert was well educated and clever. Elizabeth called Robert her "Sweet Robin" and kept him at court near her.

ROBERT DUDLEY

But Elizabeth and Robert remained friends, and Robert married someone else.

The Privy Council had another strong reason for wanting Elizabeth to marry. They wanted her to have a child—an heir. With no heir, Elizabeth could die and leave England in a power struggle. So as the queen grew older, the Privy Council grew more worried. Who would rule after Elizabeth died?

Chapter 6
A Brush with Death

In 1562, the queen got sick—very sick. Elizabeth's face broke out in small white bumps—the telltale signs of smallpox. Until a vaccine was discovered in the nineteenth century, smallpox was often fatal. Those who survived it often had terrible scars from the disease. When her doctor diagnosed smallpox, the queen screamed that she wanted another doctor. She was terrified.

During the 1500s, people did not live nearly as long as they do today. Because doctors did not understand about germs and bacteria, illnesses spread quickly. And because doctors did not have modern medicines, many common illnesses resulted in the death of the patient.

THE PLAGUE

IN 1563, A DEADLY DISEASE, KNOWN AS THE PLAGUE, BROKE OUT IN LONDON. THE PLAGUE HAD STRUCK BEFORE AND STRUCK AGAIN WHILE ELIZABETH WAS QUEEN. IT WAS ALSO CALLED THE BLACK DEATH BECAUSE ONE OF ITS SYMPTOMS WAS HORRIBLE, BLUE-BLACK SORES. FROM 1347-1351, THE SICKNESS WIPED OUT ONE-QUARTER OF EUROPE'S POPULATION.

IN TOWNS AND CITIES WHERE PEOPLE LIVED CLOSE TOGETHER, THE DISEASE SPREAD FASTER THAN IN THE COUNTRY. THERE WERE EPIDEMICS OF THE PLAGUE IN LONDON WHILE ELIZABETH WAS QUEEN. DURING THE OUTBREAKS, THE QUEEN FLED TO THE COUNTRYSIDE. THERE WAS NO CURE, NOR DID ANYONE KNOW ITS CAUSE. (NOW WE KNOW FLEAS ON INFECTED RATS SPREAD THE PLAGUE.)

DEATH WAS SUCH A PART OF LIFE THAT A POPULAR CHILDREN'S NURSERY RHYME FROM THE 1600S, "RING-A-RING O' ROSES," IS THOUGHT

TO BE ABOUT THE PLAGUE! THE "RING-A-
RING O' ROSES" DESCRIBES THE SPOTS THAT
APPEARED ON A VICTIM'S SKIN. THE "POCKETFUL
OF POSIES" REFERS TO THE BOUQUETS OF
FLOWERS THAT PEOPLE CARRIED AROUND TO
MASK THE SMELL OF DEAD BODIES.

With no cure for smallpox, Elizabeth's doctors were helpless, and so were her advisers. The days went by and she did not get better. The Privy Council called an emergency meeting. Who would take the throne if she died?

Robert Dudley assembled an army of six thousand soldiers to guard the castle. If word got out about the queen's illness, there could be a rebellion.

The doctor then decided to wrap the queen in yards and yards of red fabric. Only her face and one of her hands were left uncovered.

When this was done, he placed Elizabeth in front of a roaring fire.

For some reason, the queen recovered. To this day, no one knows why. And no one knows for sure if Elizabeth was scarred from the disease. (A lady-in-waiting caught smallpox from the queen and had such terrible scars that she never let anyone see her again.)

As she grew older, Elizabeth wore heavy white makeup. Perhaps this was to cover up the scars. However, no one really knows. All paintings of the queen done after her illness still show her with flawless skin.

Only thirty, the queen had survived a brush with death. Now more than ever, her Privy Council wanted to have someone next in line for the throne of England.

And, not far away, in Scotland, another queen had her eyes on Elizabeth's throne, too.

Chapter 7
The Queen's Cousin

Although Scotland occupies the same island as England and is now part of Great Britain, in Elizabeth's time it was a separate country. The two nations had a difficult relationship. Again and again England tried to take over Scotland. For years, the Scottish looked for help from France, England's great rival, to keep English invaders at bay.

Not long after Elizabeth became queen of England, Mary Stuart became ruler of Scotland. She was known as Mary, Queen of Scots. Mary and Elizabeth were distant cousins. But they were far from friends.

Because Mary Stuart was related to King Henry the Eighth, she had a claim to the English throne. Also, Mary Stuart was Catholic. Many Catholics in England wanted Mary, a Catholic, and not Elizabeth, sitting on the English throne. They thought that Mary Stuart was England's rightful leader. And it seemed that Mary thought so, too! She signed her letters with a special seal—it had her family's coat of

MARY, QUEEN OF SCOTS

arms joined with England's royal coat of arms. Mary was an attractive woman, who, it was rumored, could use her charms to convince anyone to do anything for her. Elizabeth worried that Mary Stuart would use the support of Catholics in England and Scotland to steal the throne.

However, Mary Stuart was not a popular queen in Scotland. She angered her people by marrying a man they did not like. The Scottish rebelled. They wanted Mary off the throne. Fearing for her life, Mary fled Scotland on horseback in the middle of the night. She rode for miles, crossing into England. Through letters, she begged her cousin Queen Elizabeth, whom she called "sister," to protect her. This made Elizabeth nervous. She didn't want Mary in England. After all, Mary had refused to recognize Elizabeth as queen.

But Elizabeth could not refuse to help another queen—a queen who was her cousin. So she agreed to keep Mary safe.

Over the next nineteen years, Mary lived in at least four different castles in England. Mary hated the cold, crumbling castles where she was kept. Different lords were in charge of guarding Mary and keeping an eye on her. Elizabeth's advisers suspected her of plotting against Queen Elizabeth.

Their suspicions were right. But often there wasn't enough solid proof against Mary Stuart.

Then, in 1586, a group of rebels planned to free Mary Stuart and put her on the throne of England. Their plan failed only because Elizabeth's faithful Walsingham got wind of it through his network of spies. This time there

was proof. Mary Stuart was smuggling notes to the rebels in beer barrels from the castle where she was held prisoner.

When Elizabeth found out, she was furious. The rebels' leader was put to death. But what would Elizabeth do about Mary? She had protected her cousin in England for almost twenty years. Now

Elizabeth looked like a fool.

Mary Stuart was put on trial. She was allowed to defend herself but was found guilty of treason. The judges sentenced Mary Stuart to death.

Although Elizabeth had no love for her cousin, she did not want to sign the death warrant. As the days went by, Elizabeth's health suffered. It was a difficult situation. If she did not execute Mary, a traitor, everyone would see her as weak. If she did, she was executing a queen.

In the end, Elizabeth signed the warrant, and Mary Stuart was beheaded. Church bells rang in celebration. (In life, Mary and Elizabeth never met face-to-face, but they are buried only a few feet from each other in Westminster Abbey.)

However, when the queen heard the bells, she went into a temper. She claimed that she had not agreed to the execution. Elizabeth wanted to deny her part in the death. Instead of taking responsibility, she could blame others.

That did little to calm King Philip of Spain. Like Mary Stuart, he was Catholic. He was furious that Elizabeth had put to death a Catholic queen. It was all the reason he needed to go to war against England.

In 1588 he sent his ships, known as the Armada, to England. The first fleet was to distract the English navy in a battle at sea so that troops in other ships could land and storm the countryside. He hoped to seize the English crown from Elizabeth.

The sea battle lasted for days. But luck was with the English. First, they burned some of the enemy ships. Then a great storm came through the

English Channel. Spanish ships crashed against the rocks and were destroyed. Desperate Spanish soldiers who swam away were killed on shore.

It was a great moment for England. The storm was seen as a blessing from God. Elizabeth had shown that she, a woman, could fight a war as well as any king. The English navy had proven itself by defeating the powerful Armada. In the coming years, England would rule the seas with its great navy.

THE SEA DOG

SIR FRANCIS DRAKE

TO THE ENGLISH, SIR FRANCIS DRAKE WAS A
HERO. TO THE SPANISH, HE WAS A LOW-LIFE PIRATE.
AN ENGLISH ADVENTURER AND SEA CAPTAIN,
DRAKE COMMANDED HIS FIRST SHIP WHEN HE WAS
TWENTY-EIGHT AND TRAVELED TO THE NEW WORLD
(AMERICA) A FEW YEARS LATER. EARLY ON, HE WAS
CAPTURED AT SEA BY THE SPANISH. HE ESCAPED,
BUT FOR THE REST OF HIS LIFE HE HATED SPAIN.
FRANCIS BECAME FAMOUS AS A "SEA DOG,"

A MAN WHOSE MISSION WAS TO DISCOVER NEW LANDS BUT ALSO PLUNDER SHIPS. SEA DOGS WERE NOT SO DIFFERENT FROM PIRATES, EXCEPT THAT A BIG PART OF THE TREASURE THEY STOLE WENT TO THE QUEEN.

IN 1580, THE QUEEN KNIGHTED DRAKE. ALTHOUGH DRAKE WAS NOT OFFICIALLY A PART OF THE BRITISH ROYAL NAVY, IN 1588 HE WAS NAMED SECOND-IN-COMMAND OF THE ENGLISH FLEET AGAINST THE SPANISH ARMADA. KING PHILIP OF SPAIN SO DESPISED DRAKE THAT HE OFFERED TWENTY THOUSAND SPANISH DUCATS (MORE THAN TEN MILLION DOLLARS!) FOR HIS HEAD.

Chapter 8
The Golden Age

Elizabeth was at the height of her popularity. Her people adored her. Artists painted the queen in all her splendor. In fact, more portraits were painted of Elizabeth than of any other ruler in

England's history. (Elizabeth had to approve every portrait; any that she did not like were destroyed.) Her likeness hung in homes and public spaces across England. Even if they had never seen her in person, English citizens knew how magnificent their Elizabeth was.

THE NEW WORLD

ELIZABETH WAS QUEEN DURING AN EXCITING TIME OF EXPLORATION.

AFTER COLUMBUS CROSSED THE ATLANTIC OCEAN IN 1492 AND LATER CLAIMED ISLANDS OFF THE COAST OF SOUTH AMERICA FOR SPAIN, OTHER COUNTRIES IN EUROPE WANTED STRONGHOLDS IN THE NEW WORLD, TOO. THEY WANTED TO CLAIM LAND AND BRING BACK RICHES—EVERYTHING FROM NEW FRUITS AND VEGETABLES TO EXOTIC ANIMALS, JEWELS, AND GOLD.

BY THE MID-1500S, EUROPEAN COLONIES TOOK ROOT IN THE NEW WORLD. THE SPANISH, FRENCH, AND ENGLISH CLAIMED TERRITORY IN WHAT IS NOW CANADA, WHAT IS NOW THE UNITED STATES, THE CARIBBEAN, AND BRAZIL. THEY TOOK LAND BELONGING TO NATIVE PEOPLES FOR THEMSELVES. THEY FELT IT WAS THEIR RIGHT.

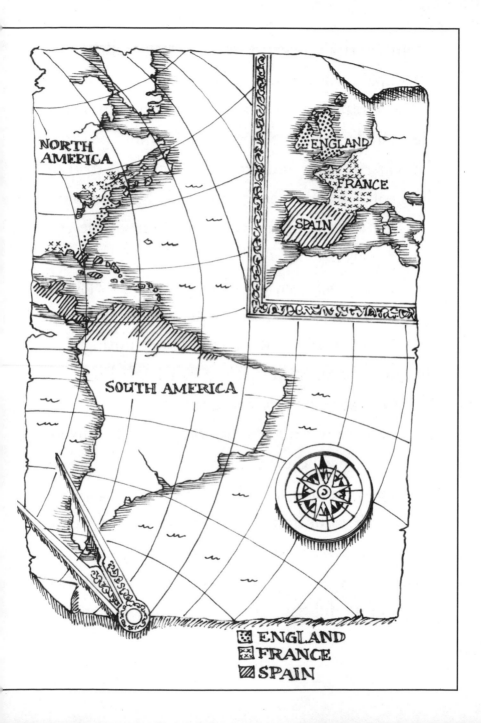

In a portrait made to celebrate England's victory over Spain, Elizabeth is shown wearing a satin and velvet gown. Perfect bows and shimmering pearls decorate her gown. She wears even more pearls in her ears and hair and around her neck. A delicate lace collar frames her face. Elizabeth's right hand rests on a globe, to show England's new role as a world power.

In the background of the painting, Spanish ships are being overtaken by the English fleet. But it is Elizabeth who is the focus of the painting. The queen looks magnificent, larger than life. Elizabeth was Gloriana, the glorious queen.

Elizabeth was quite a fashion plate! The queen's style influenced the way ladies at her court dressed. Of course, no one would dare outshine the queen. Fashion became much fancier—ruffs around the neck and wrists became bigger, and skirts and sleeves grew wider and wider. Fabric was covered in patterns and trimmed with braids and jewels.

THE QUEEN'S WARDROBE

ELIZABETH OWNED HUNDREDS OF DRESSES.
EACH WAS LIKE A FANTASTIC COSTUME.
ELIZABETH NEEDED HELP PUTTING ON THE HEAVY
GOWNS, WHICH HAD EIGHT LAYERS. SHE COULD
HAVE NEVER DRESSED HERSELF!

FIRST, CAME THE BODICE. THE BODICE WAS
MADE OF WHALEBONES, WOOD, OR STEEL, AND
FASTENED WITH RIBBONS THAT LACED IN THE
BACK. IT SQUEEZED IN A WOMAN'S STOMACH
AND MADE HER WAIST SMALLER. (BODICES FOR
ORDINARY WOMEN WERE LOOSER SO THE WOMEN
COULD DO THEIR CHORES.)

NEXT CAME THE PETTICOATS. A PETTICOAT
IS LIKE A SKIRT WITH EXTRA LAYERS. IT IS
WORN UNDERNEATH A DRESS FOR A FULLER
SHAPE. SOMETIMES A SERIES OF HOOPS HAD
TO BE WORN TO SUPPORT SKIRTS MADE OF THE
HEAVIEST FABRICS.

THEN CAME THE GOWN. HER GOWNS WERE
MADE OUT OF BEAUTIFUL FABRICS FROM ALL
OVER EUROPE, IN SPLENDID COLORS AND HAND
EMBROIDERED. GLITTERING JEWELS WERE SEWN
ONTO THEM.

FINALLY, ELABORATE RUFFS WERE PLACED AROUND THE QUEEN'S NECK AND AROUND HER WRISTS.

WHEN THE QUEEN ENTERED A ROOM, EVERYONE AT COURT FELL SILENT. AND WHEN THE QUEEN APPEARED BEFORE HER PEOPLE, CROWDS WOULD GASP IN AWE.

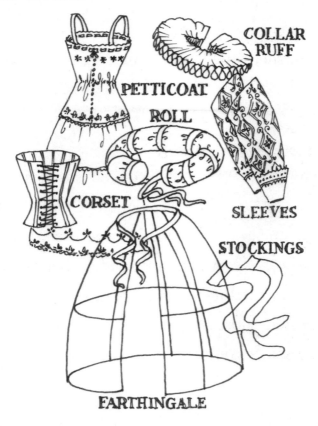

COLLAR
RUFF

PETTICOAT

ROLL

CORSET

SLEEVES

STOCKINGS

FARTHINGALE

Men's style became fancier, too. Pants were wider and puffier. Men at court dyed their hair to match their outfits. Some men wore girdles, for a slimmer waist! The courtiers presented the queen with jewels— rubies and pearls—and flattered her, saying the jewels matched "the life of your eyes and the color of your lips." These gifts made the queen feel like a goddess, beautiful and forever young.

The queen also enjoyed music, dancing, and theater. Elizabeth loved the arts more than any ruler before her. She was an intelligent, well-read woman, and she expected those around her to keep up with her interests. If you wanted to impress the queen, you had to read important works of literature, know about drama and the latest plays, and sing and dance well. You might even have been expected to recite a sonnet for Her Majesty right on the spot! At court, musicians and actors performed for Elizabeth's entertainment.

Outside of Whitehall Palace, in London, playwrights like Christopher Marlowe and William Shakespeare grew popular. The first theater was built in 1586.

The famous Globe Theatre was built in 1599 by William Shakespeare for his plays. Now even members of the lower classes

CHRISTOPHER MARLOWE

could attend a play. Although brutal sports like bearbaiting and cockfighting were still popular, people were also finding entertainment in new stories, plays, dances, and music.

WILLIAM SHAKESPEARE

WILLIAM SHAKESPEARE

WILLIAM SHAKESPEARE WAS BORN IN 1564 (NO ONE KNOWS THE EXACT DAY) IN THE SMALL TOWN OF STRATFORD, JUST NORTH OF LONDON. HE WAS THE THIRD OF EIGHT CHILDREN, AND HIS FATHER WAS A GLOVER. THE SHAKESPEARES WERE NEITHER RICH NOR POOR. WILLIAM ONLY WENT TO SCHOOL FOR A FEW YEARS, BUT HE GREW UP TO BECOME ENGLAND'S GREATEST POET AND PLAYWRIGHT.

SHAKESPEARE WROTE MORE THAN 35 PLAYS IN HIS LIFETIME, INCLUDING *ROMEO AND JULIET*, *HAMLET*, *OTHELLO*, *MACBETH*, *A MIDSUMMER NIGHT'S DREAM*, AND *RICHARD III*, AND MORE THAN 150 SONNETS. SHAKESPEARE WAS POPULAR IN HIS OWN TIME BECAUSE HIS PLAYS WERE ENTERTAINING, MOVING, AND FUNNY ALL AT ONCE. BOTH THE NOBILITY AND THE COMMON PEOPLE ENJOYED THEM. ELIZABETH HERSELF WAS A

GREAT FAN OF SHAKESPEARE'S PLAYS. AS AN ACTOR, SHAKESPEARE AND HIS TROUPE, THE LORD CHAMBERLAIN'S MEN, WERE INVITED TO PERFORM FOR HER MAJESTY! WILL PROBABLY ADMIRED THE QUEEN, TOO. SOME PEOPLE THINK THE INTELLIGENT, FIERY HEROINE IN *THE TAMING OF THE SHREW* WAS BASED ON QUEEN ELIZABETH.

TODAY, SHAKESPEARE'S PLAYS ARE PERFORMED MORE THAN ANYONE ELSE'S IN THE WORLD. THE WAY WE SPEAK AND READ THE ENGLISH LANGUAGE MAY HAVE CHANGED SINCE SHAKESPEARE'S TIME, BUT HIS PLAYS ABOUT POWER, FALLEN HEROES, LOVE, AND TRAGEDY STILL MOVE AUDIENCES TO THIS DAY.

Chapter 9
Death of a Queen

In 1600, Elizabeth was sixty-seven years old. She still enjoyed walking outdoors and she rode her favorite horses—Grey Pool and Black Wilford— almost every day.

At parties, she made a point of dancing so that members of the court would see that their queen was still lively and energetic. Often, the queen tired out many young partygoers.

Elizabeth had ruled for forty-one years.

However, the last years of her rule were difficult ones for the country and its queen.

For a long time, the yearly harvest had been poor. Famine was killing off people. Those who survived were hungry and angry. The poor left the countryside and crowded the streets of London. There was unrest. Could it lead to rebellion?

EARL OF ESSEX

The question of who would rule after Elizabeth became ever more urgent. But the queen put off choosing anyone. It meant thinking about her own death. Even worse, it meant thinking of someone else ruling *her* country.

No one else could love *her* people as she had.

But the heaviest blow of all was personal. Someone Elizabeth loved had betrayed her.

After Robert Dudley (Sweet Robin) died, Elizabeth became close to his adopted son, the Earl of Essex. She put him in charge of her horses. The Earl of Essex soon became a favorite of the queen.

Essex was charming and handsome, but he was also greedy. He wanted to run the wine trade. When

Elizabeth said no, he insulted her in front of the Privy Council. The friendship was shattered.

For weeks, Essex wrote to the queen, begging forgiveness. In one letter he said that until he saw her again, "time itself is a perpetual night."

Elizabeth, however, would not forgive him. Once out of favor, Essex was ruined. He owed people money—a lot of money—and now he had no way to pay off his debts. Pressure on him was mounting. People said he began acting like a crazy person. Foolishly, he began insulting the queen again.

Essex convinced himself Elizabeth was not ruling wisely, that she was leading England into danger. In time, Essex began to believe that he should rule instead of Elizabeth.

With a group of supporters, Essex hatched an outrageous plot: His men would break into the castle where Elizabeth was staying and make her call a meeting with parliament. She would

be forced to name Essex Lord Protector. As Lord Protector he would be in charge, not Elizabeth.

Essex managed to assemble two hundred soldiers. But he wanted the people of London to support the rebellion. He stormed through London's taverns, his sword raised high, yelling and trying to rally support for his cause.

Essex badly misjudged Londoners. They would

not join his rebellion. They were loyal to their queen.

William Cecil's spies had gotten advance word of the plot. The queen's men were ready for Essex and his band of rebels as they approached the castle. Essex fled but was soon arrested and found guilty of high treason. The court sentenced him to death. The queen had no second thoughts about signing the death warrant. (The death warrant can still be seen today, on display in the British Library.) In February 1601, Essex was beheaded.

Despite his treachery, Elizabeth mourned the Earl of Essex. For the rest of her life, she wore a ring he had given her. For months after his death, she remained depressed. She would stay in her bedroom. It was hard for her to focus; she grew weaker. Her zest for life was gone.

In September, the queen turned sixty-nine. And now she seemed her age. She no longer enjoyed dancing. Her eyesight was failing. Letters had to be read to her.

In November 1601, the queen gave her final speech to parliament. Her robes seemed to weigh her down, and she had to struggle to sit tall. But when the queen spoke, she was as majestic and regal as ever. She declared her love for the English people, saying that their loyalty meant more than the most expensive jewels. She said, "You may have many a wiser prince sitting in this seat, but you never have had, or shall have, any who loves you better."

Before she took her leave, trumpets sounded. And the queen allowed all 150 members to kiss her hand.

After that, Elizabeth grew steadily weaker. She needed a cane to walk up and down the stairs. Once, before a meeting, she almost collapsed under the weight of her heavy robes. In 1602, the English fleet captured a Portuguese ship and brought treasure back to their queen. But Elizabeth was not as excited at the news of riches as she once might have been. Now, it was almost impossible to please the queen. Her beloved Robin had died and the Earl of Essex had betrayed her. Even her right-hand man, William Cecil, had passed away. The queen felt alone and was full of despair.

In March of 1603, the queen retired to her private rooms. For days, she paced about nervously. She would not sleep. She did not eat. For two days straight, she stood and stared out her bedroom window, without once sitting down.

She could not speak because of pain in her throat. A doctor who examined her found her throat filled with sores. Finally, she lay down in bed. Clearly the end was near. Now she had to face the question that she had dodged for so long: Who would rule after her? Although unable to speak, Elizabeth let her advisers know her choice.

It was James the Sixth, king of Scotland—and the son of her old enemy Mary Stuart.

On March 24, in the early morning hours, the queen died. People were stunned as news spread of the queen's death. Many had never lived under any other

KING JAMES

ruler. James, the new king, paid for an elaborate and expensive funeral. Drawn by a team of horses in black, Elizabeth's coffin was draped in purple velvet. (Purple is the color for royalty.) Over a

thousand of the queen's subjects, from maids to noblemen, followed behind.

Queen Elizabeth was laid to rest in Westminster Abbey. And who was she placed right next to in the cathedral? Her half-sister Mary, who had put Elizabeth in prison so many years ago!

The young girl who had been shunned by her father had grown to become one of England's greatest rulers. She had lived in a world where men were thought to be smarter, wiser, and better in all ways than women. She had led the English navy to victory, and encouraged the growth of literature and the arts, and in the end she had left her people with a great gift: a strong and powerful England.

LONDON

DURING THE TIME OF ELIZABETH I, MOST PEOPLE IN ENGLAND LIVED ON FARMS IN THE COUNTRYSIDE, BUT LONDON, THE CAPITAL CITY, WAS GROWING—FAST. BY 1600, APPROXIMATELY 200,000 PEOPLE LIVED THERE. LONDON WAS BUSY AND NOISY; ITS STREETS WERE CROWDED WITH PEOPLE BUYING AND SELLING EVERYTHING FROM TURNIPS, COAL, AND WOOD TO PEACOCKS! TRAVELING ACTORS PERFORMED IN THE STREETS;

THE POOR BEGGED FOR MONEY. LONDON BRIDGE,
WHICH CROSSED THE THAMES RIVER, WAS
CRAMMED WITH STORES AND WOODEN HOUSES.

LONDONERS HAD TO WORK HARD TO MAKE ENDS
MEET. BUT THEY ENJOYED WHAT LITTLE FREE TIME
THEY HAD. CROWDS ATTENDED EVENTS CALLED
"BULL" OR "BEARBAITING." BEARS OR BULLS WERE
TIED UP AND ATTACKED BY DOGS. IT WAS VIOLENT
AND CRUEL, BUT VERY POPULAR BACK THEN.

Chapter 10
Another Elizabeth

In Great Britain today, there is still a queen. And her name is Elizabeth. In 1952, she became Queen Elizabeth II. Like Elizabeth I, no one expected Elizabeth II to become queen. Her uncle had been the king. Everyone thought his sons would rule after him. But in 1936, Elizabeth's uncle gave up the throne to marry a divorced commoner. So Elizabeth's father became king. After his death, Elizabeth took the throne.

On the day she was crowned in 1953, Elizabeth II wore a long robe and heavy crown just like Queen Elizabeth I. Her gown was embroidered with the Tudor rose, the flower that was the symbol of the first Queen Elizabeth's family. But there the similarities end.

Today parliament—the government—makes all the laws in Great Britain. Queen Elizabeth II is the head of state, but she has no real power.

Still, Queen Elizabeth II is important. She meets regularly with the prime minister, the head of parliament, and is kept informed on important issues. She presides over countless ceremonies, and she grants honors such as knighthood.

Unlike Elizabeth I, Elizabeth II is married and has four grown children. The oldest, Prince Charles, is next in line for the throne. Prince Charles has been waiting to become king for a long time. His mother is over eighty but in good health. She has been queen for more than fifty years and is one of the longest ruling heads of state in the world! The queen has said that she will not retire but will remain on the throne for the rest of her life.

Prince Charles has two sons, William and Henry (everyone calls him Harry). They are second and third in line to the throne. In 1997, the boys' mother, the popular Princess Diana, died in a terrible car crash. Since then, William and Harry have worked hard to continue their mother's legacy of working for charities and visiting poor nations around the world.

In Britain today, some people think that having a king or queen and a royal family is too old-fashioned. Recently, the British people opposed a tax to help pay for repairs on one of the royal castles. Why, many thought, should the average citizen pay for the royal family's rich lifestyle? But to other people, the royal family is important. Though elected officials come and go, the queen and her family remain a link to the past and Great Britain's long history.

TIMELINE OF
QUEEN ELIZABETH'S LIFE

1533 —— Elizabeth is born in Greenwich, England

1536 —— Execution of Elizabeth's mother, Anne Boleyn;
Henry marries Jane Seymour

1553 —— Mary Tudor becomes Queen of England

1559 —— Elizabeth is crowned Queen of England

1563 —— Plague epidemic in London

1580 —— Sir Francis Drake becomes the first Englishman
to sail around the world

1582 —— Plague occurs again in London

1587 —— Execution of Mary, Queen of Scots

1588 —— The Spanish Armada is defeated by the English

1590 —— Death of Sir Francis Walsingham

1592 —— Another epidemic of plague in London

1598 —— Death of William Cecil

1601 —— Earl of Essex is executed

1603 —— Queen Elizabeth dies;
King James is crowned

TIMELINE OF THE WORLD

Death of King Henry's third wife, Jane Seymour — **1537**

Henry marries and divorces Anne of Cleves — **1540**

Catherine Howard, Henry's fifth wife, is executed — **1542**

Henry marries Catherine Parr, his sixth and last wife, who outlives him — **1543**

Martin Luther dies — **1546**

King Henry dies — **1547**

Michelangelo dies in Rome; the astronomer Galileo is born — **1564**

James (the future king of England) is born in Scotland — **1566**

More than 6,000 French Protestants are executed in France — **1572**

Shakespeare writes *Romeo and Juliet* — **1594**

The Globe Theatre opens in London — **1599**

Jamestown settlement in the colony of Virginia is founded — **1607**

William Shakespeare dies — **1616**

BIBLIOGRAPHY

Havelin, Kate. **Queen Elizabeth I.** Lerner Publications, Minnesota, 2002.

Roberts, Chris. **Heavy Words Lightly Thrown: The Reason Behind the Rhyme.** Gotham Books, New York, 2005.

Singman, Jeffrey L. **Daily Life in Elizabethan England.** Greenwood Press, Connecticut, 1995.

Somerset, Anne. **Elizabeth I.** Anchor Books, New York; 2003.

Stanley, Diane, and Peter Vennema. **Good Queen Bess: The Story of Elizabeth I of England.** HarperCollins, New York, 2001.

Starkey, David. **Elizabeth: The Struggle for the Throne.** HarperCollins, New York, 2001.

Thomas, Jane Resh. **Behind the Mask: The Life of Queen Elizabeth I.** Clarion Books, New York, 1998.

Weir, Alison. **The Life of Elizabeth I.** Ballantine, New York, 1998.

Website:

Elizabeth R. by Heather Thomas:
www.elizabethi.org